CatDala
COLORING BOOK

Over 50 Cat Mandalas for inspiration, mindfulness, and fun

Laurren Darr

Text and illustrations copyright © 2016 Laurren Darr /Left Paw Press

All rights reserved. No part of this book may be reproduced or transmitted in any form or by any means, electronic or mechanical, including photocopying, recording, or by an information storage retrieval system, without express written permission from the publisher.

Left Paw Press

Contact us on our publisher's website at:
www.LeftPawPress.com

International Standard Book Number: 978-1-943356-23-2

PRINTED IN THE UNITED STATES OF AMERICA

Author: Laurren Darr

Cover design by Maria Charina Gomez.

Published and distributed by Left Paw Press, publishing imprint of Lauren Originals, Inc. For educational, corporate, or retail sales accounts, email: info@LeftPawPress.com.

For information, address: Left Paw Press, c/o Lauren Originals, Inc. 8926 N Greenwood Avenue #293 Niles, IL 60714. Left Paw Press can be found on the web at www.leftpawpress.com.

Advantages of coloring

Many promising studies have been conducted on art therapy. For those who are less inclined to create art as therapy and wanting a simpler solution, they are using coloring books to enrich their lives. Physicians and therapists prescribe coloring for many different illnesses including depression, PTSD, dementia, and even cancer patients to reduce their pain and stress levels in treatment.

Everyday, people are also looking for natural and joyful ways to lessen pain and reduce the tension in their lives. By coloring, the mind focuses. This, in turn, allows the brain to replace mind chatter and negative thoughts with positive thoughts. There are many benefits to having a coloring book routine, which include:

• Achieve a meditation state of mind. The alpha brain waves are present when the mind is sleeping or in a deep zen-like meditative state. When a person is coloring, the brain can get into this soothing, restorative mode.

• Assuage stress, worry, and fears. This happens in the amygdala portion of the brain where emotions and motivation are integrated. The amygdala gets calmed during the coloring process.

• Improve fine motor skills. This happens through the repetition of coloring and focusing on a task using your hands to stay within a finite area.

• Increase creativity. Coloring unlocks the right side of the brain and keeps it stimulated, allowing for more creative thoughts and solutions. This also leads to increased productivity.

• Relax, gain clarity, and focus. People can also reduce their blood pressure while coloring.

How to use this book

First of all, there is no wrong way of using this book to bring more peace to your life. There also is no right or wrong time or place to color. Taking the time to include creativity in your life will help with your well-being. This is the vision that I had when I set out to create the *PugDala Coloring Book*. I wanted it to be of optimal benefit to anyone that got a copy. With that being said, onward!

Gather your materials. There is no particular medium to use. If you're drawn to colored pencils, crayons, markers, or paint, go with the flow. You may also decide to use different materials at different times. I have a long desk in my office that has a mixture of all of these. I grab whatever 'strikes my fancy.'

Thumb through the PugDalas and pick one that piques your interest. Some people like to keep the book together and others like to cut the page out to color it. Again, it's whatever works best for you. It's also appropriate to note that it doesn't matter whether you complete the PugDala or not. Color until you feel 'complete.'

You'll also find that, the pages opposite the PugDalas have a mantra. These affirmations are included as a suggestion to meditate on while coloring. You'll find that they are repeated in the background to represent how people mentally repeat a mantra over and over. These are also faded so that you can include your own colored notes on what that PugDala and mantra brought up for you. However, if this isn't something that doesn't resonate with you, no worries. I can't stress enough to follow your energy and color in a way that feels best and is most appealing to you.

Most importantly, have fun coloring, relaxing, and taking time to include creativity in your life! Allow the *PugDala Coloring Book* to bring you joy!

Lauren

I am at peace...

I love and accept myself completely...

I allow myself to dream...

I am surrounded by love...

I am healthy, wealthy, and wise...

I choose happiness...

I love my life...

I am open...

I deserve all that is good in the world...

I am in the flow...

I bring love and joy to everything I do...

I am confident

I am free to make my own choices and decisions...

I am calm...

I am successful...

I am healthy and balanced...

I honor myself at all times...

I have been blessed in this body...

I learn from all of my experiences...

I am grateful for everything in my life...

I value myself...

I am a magnet for miracles...

I release all worries...

I am proud of myself...

I am worthy...

I choose prosperity...

I am more than enough... just as I am...

I am safe and secure...

I appreciate all of my experiences...

I trust my higher self...

I am financially secure...

I am alive and filled with vitality...

I radiate love and joy to everyone I meet...

I nourish myself...

I have an open mind...

I deserve a happy and prosperous life...

I believe in unlimited possibilities…

I am the creator of my success...

I am all that I can be...

I feel oneness with all of life...

I love today...
It is a great
day...

I am a blessing...

I am filled with pure positive energy...

I am motivated to reach my goals...

I deserve to be financially free and independent...

I am worthy of prosperity, joy, and love...

I attract all things that I desire in my life....

I possess the wisdom and power to accomplish anything...

I hold the keys to my destiny...

I have fun all the time...

I am beautiful...

I forgive any and all debt owed to me...

I speak my truth...

PUG CHILDREN'S FAIRY TALE SERIES
BOOKS ARE AVAILABLE IN
COLOR AND COLORING BOOK VERSIONS

LEFT PAW Press

www.LeftPawPress.com

LEFT PAW Press

PROUDLY PUBLISHES MEDICAL BOOKS BY DR. BRAD T. TINKLE

www.LeftPawPress.com

About The Author

Laurren Darr has been 'owned' by pets since her first pug rescue of White Pines Tuttie when she was just six years old. Tuttie had never been out of a cage or even uttered a bark. She was the joy of Laurren's life until she left this world at the age of 15 (human years, of course!). This silly pug would let Laurren dress her, put clippy earrings on her, and even put lipstick on her. They'd spend hours tootling around the neighborhood dressed in their Sunday best, which is why Tuttie served as the inspiration for the launch of the International Association of Pet Fashion Professionals over thirty years later.

Laurren also had her first cat – a black beauty with green eyes that she named Kitty Cat Darr. Her next cat was a feral neighborhood cat named Tigger.

Laurren has had many pugs since. Zacchaeus was a gift to her for her 16th birthday. She has also featured family rescue pugs Inky & Sarge (brother and sister) and Benji, in other Pug Fairy Tale Series story adaptations.

Laurren's busy Chicago-area home is filled with her husband, her son, and a fabulously fashionable pug named Bella.

www.ingramcontent.com/pod-product-compliance
Lightning Source LLC
Chambersburg PA
CBHW080923170426

43201CB00016B/2251